Florence Nightingale

John Malam

Heinemann
LIBRARY

www.heinemann.co.uk
Visit our website to find out more information about **Heinemann Library** books.

To order:
☎ Phone 44 (0) 1865 888066
▤ Send a fax to 44 (0) 1865 314091
▢ Visit the Heinemann Bookshop at www.heinemann.co.uk to browse our catalogue and order online.

Produced by Monkey Puzzle Media Ltd,
Gissing's Farm, Fressingfield, Suffolk IP21 5SH, UK

First published in Great Britain by Heinemann Library,
Halley Court, Jordan Hill, Oxford OX2 8EJ,
a division of Reed Educational and Professional Publishing Ltd.
Heinemann is a registered trademark of Reed Educational and Professional Publishing Ltd.

OXFORD MELBOURNE AUCKLAND
JOHANNESBURG BLANTYRE GABORONE
IBADAN PORTSMOUTH (NH) USA CHICAGO

Designed by Tessa Barwick
Illustrated by Michael Posen
Originated by Ambassador Litho Ltd
Printed in Hong Kong

ISBN 0 431 10479 4 (hardback)   ISBN 0 431 10486 7 (paperback)
05 04 03 02   06 05 04 03 02
10 9 8 7 6 5 4 3 2   10 9 8 7 6 5 4 3 2 1

British Library Cataloguing in Publication Data
Malam, John
  Florence Nightingale. - (Groundbreakers)
  1.Nightingale, Florence, 1820-1910 - Juvenile literature
  2.Nurses - England - Biography - Juvenile literature
  3.Crimean War, 1853-1856 - Medical care - Great Britain - Juvenile literature
  I.Title
  610.7'3'092

Acknowledgements
The publishers would like to thank the following for permission to reproduce photographs: Art Archive 28; Bridgeman Art Library 12/Royal Holloway and Bedford New College, Surrey, UK; The Florence Nightingale Museum 4, 5, 6, 9, 10, 14, 22, 24, 25 top and bottom, 30, 31, 32, 33, 34, 35, 36, 37, 38, 39, 40, 41; Hulton Getty 7, 8, 19, 26, 27; John and Hilary Malam 15, 29; Mary Evans Picture Library 17, 20, 23; MPM Images 16; National Portrait Gallery 11; P&O Art Collection 21; Science Photo Library 42/James King-Holmes, 43/Simon Fraser; Wellcome Library, London 13.

Cover photograph reproduced with the permission of Mary Evans Picture Library.

Every effort has been made to contact copyright holders of any material reproduced in this book. Any omissions will be rectified in subsequent printings if notice is given to the publishers.

Any words appearing in the text in bold, **like this**, are explained in the glossary.

Contents

Who was Florence Nightingale?

The world is the way it is because of what people have done in the past. Our lives have been changed by inventions and discoveries. However, these are not the only things that have shaped our world. One of the greatest ways society develops is by changing the way we think about something, and the people who succeed in bringing about change are called **reformers**.

A great reformer

One such reformer was Florence Nightingale, a British woman who lived in the 1800s. From an early age Florence felt she had been called by God to work among the poor and the sick. Her parents were horrified when she told them she wanted to become a nurse. At the time, nursing was not a respectable occupation for women who, like Florence, came from good families. However, she was determined to follow her calling, not the wishes of her parents. Eventually, she did become a nurse.

This painting from 1855 shows Florence Nightingale visiting soldiers in hospital during the Crimean War.

A turning point

Wars, dreadful though they are, change society. For example, the American Civil War led to the abolition of slavery in America; World War II led to the redrawing of the map of Europe. A war was also the turning point in Florence Nightingale's life. In the mid-1850s Britain was at war in the Crimea, a region in southern Russia. Florence went there with a group of nurses. She cared for sick and wounded soldiers, and improved the conditions of the military hospitals there.

In Britain, after the war, Florence set up the Nightingale Training School. It taught women about nursing and trained them to be nurses. She wrote a groundbreaking book that described how she thought nursing should be done. Little by little, Florence laid the foundations for nursing as we know it today.

This photograph of Florence Nightingale was taken in 1856, when she was 36 years old.

THE LADY WITH A LAMP

In 1857 the American poet Henry Longfellow (1807–82) wrote a poem about Florence Nightingale. Here is one of its verses:

Lo! in that house of misery
A lady with a lamp I see
Pass through the glimmering gloom,
And flit from room to room.

Longfellow's poem described Florence as 'a lady with a lamp'. Ever since, this is how she has been remembered, walking the dark corridors and gloomy wards of her battlefield hospital, the way ahead lit by the flickering light of a lamp.

Florence Nightingale was a remarkable woman. She worked hard to overcome the **prejudices** people had about nursing, and about the role of women in British society. Her gift to the present-day world is something we cannot now live without – nursing is accepted as an essential part of modern society.

Florence is born

In the early years of the 19th century it was fashionable for wealthy British people to travel to the cities of Europe. The tourists of the early 1800s did not just visit these places for a few weeks like today's holiday-makers, they remained overseas for months, and even years at a time.

Florence's parents in Italy

Florence Nightingale's life story begins on just such a foreign trip. In 1818, her parents, William and Frances Nightingale, left Britain to visit Italy. They were wealthy, and as neither of them had to work for a living they could stay away from Britain for a long time, if they wanted to. In Italy, the Nightingales visited ancient ruins, and churches adorned with wonderful paintings. For the newly-married couple this was a chance to see famous works of art and architecture at first hand.

William and Frances Nightingale, Florence's parents. This photograph shows them in their old age.

FLORENCE'S PARENTS

Florence's father was born William Edward Shore (1794–1874). When he was a boy, William inherited a fortune from his great-uncle, Peter Nightingale. He also inherited land in Derbyshire, a county in the middle of England. The money and the land became William's when he was 21. In honour of his generous relative, William changed his last name from Shore to Nightingale. Had William not done this, Florence Nightingale would have been Florence Shore.

Florence's mother was Frances Smith (1788–1880), known to everyone as Fanny. She was one of ten children and was the daughter of a politician. She had a **privileged** upbringing, mixing with rich and successful people and enjoying a fine lifestyle.

An unusual name

In 1819, William and Frances were staying in Naples, a city in southern Italy. It was here that their first child was born. They named the baby girl Parthenope, which was the ancient Greek name for Naples, her birthplace. It was an unusual name, and it was often shortened to Parthe or Pop.

The following year the family travelled to the north of Italy where they rented a house on the outskirts of the city of Florence. It was here that their second daughter was born, on 12 May 1820. Like Parthenope, this girl was also named after the city of her birth, and this is how Florence Nightingale got her first name. It, too, was an unusual name at the time, and it was not long before people began to call her Flo, for short.

Florence, the Italian city where Florence Nightingale was born. This is how it looked in the early 1800s.

At home in England

In 1821, when Florence was 1 year old, her family left Italy. They had lived there for almost three years. Florence's father would have been happy to stay in Italy for longer, but her mother felt it was time they returned home to England.

Florence, aged about 16, seated and stitching embroidery, with her sister Parthenope.

Two homes

Florence's father had inherited an old house from his great-uncle, Peter Nightingale. The house at Lea, near the small town of Matlock in Derbyshire was in poor condition, and not suitable for the Nightingale family, their maids, footmen, coachmen and cook. Instead, Florence's father had a new house built nearby. It was called Lea Hurst. No sooner had the family moved in than Florence's mother realized it was a mistake. Lea Hurst would not make a good family home after all. It was a long way from London and she was worried that no one would visit. Even though the house had fifteen bedrooms she thought it was too small. Worse still, it was cold, and both Florence and Parthenope became ill with **bronchitis**. In 1825, when Florence was 5 years old, her father bought Embley Park, a house near Romsey in Hampshire. This house was closer to London, and was much better for the family.

In Nightingale's words:

'I craved for some regular occupation, for something worth doing instead of frittering [wasting] time away on useless trifles [unimportant things].'

(From a private note. Florence jotted down many of her thoughts throughout her life. These 'private notes' provide us with a real insight to her private life.)

Embley Park, the family home in Hampshire. This picture was drawn by Parthenope, who was a talented artist.

Florence's childhood

In summer, Florence lived with her family at Lea Hurst. Embley Park was the family home in winter. There were visits to London, cousins came to stay, she dressed well and ate good food. Florence should have been overjoyed at this fortunate lifestyle, but in later life she said that she had disliked it.

Like many girls from respectable families at the time, Florence and her sister Parthe were educated at home. A **governess** taught them music and drawing, and from the age of 12 their father taught them Greek, Latin, German, French, Italian, grammar, history, mathematics and **philosophy**. Parthe preferred being in the garden with her mother instead of doing schoolwork with her father. Florence was a good pupil. She particularly enjoyed mathematics. When she became a teenager, people noticed that she did not like to mix with others. Instead, she preferred to be on her own, free to drift off into a secret dream-world. She also developed a passion for neatness and accuracy. A visitor once said that Florence was 'extraordinary', which suggests that even at this age there was something different, something special about her.

EDUCATION AT THE TIME

During the early 1800s, children with wealthy parents were usually educated at home. Boys and girls were taught different things. For example, boys learned to read and write Latin and Greek, whereas girls were given piano, singing and sewing lessons. Some boys were sent to schools where they lived and studied. Children from poor families had little education. They went to work from as young as 6, unable to read and write.

Called by God

Florence as a young woman, with her pet owl, Athena, drawn by Parthenope.

Florence was becoming a woman. She was attractive and well educated, and her parents were sure she would one day make a fine wife. They started to plan her future, and as was customary for the time they prepared for her '**coming out**'. This involved holding house-parties, dinners and balls in their house at Embley Park. Florence would be introduced to the guests. It was a way of showing that she was no longer a child. But Florence still held on to things that adults thought of as childish. She had not grown out of her habit of day-dreaming. If anything, her dream-world had become more important to her. It felt real, not one she conjured up in her mind.

'COMING OUT'

For many years it was the custom in Britain for girls from well-off families to 'come out'. Each year there was a season of social events, such as dances and parties. Girls, most aged about 18, attended these events where they were presented to the host. It was an important occasion in the girls' lives — they had 'come out' of childhood and were now adults.

Voices in her head

On 7 February 1837, when Florence was at home at Embley Park she had an experience that was to change the course of her life. She had what can only be described as a mystical experience. Perhaps she had drifted into her private world of dreams. She believed she heard voices in her head calling to her. Florence thought that this was a sign from God, and that He had chosen her for a purpose.

Whatever that purpose was, it was not made clear to Florence at that time. She was 16, a young woman with the rest of her life ahead of her.

Admirers

Florence had several admirers. Henry Nicholson, one of her cousins, fell in love with her. But despite having many things in common, such as a love of mathematics, Florence had no intention of marrying him. In 1842 she met Richard Monckton Milnes. Eleven years older than Florence, he was rich, intelligent and fun to be with. They were well matched and they loved each other, but marriage was out of the question for Florence. She believed that to do God's work – whatever that was going to be – she must remain unmarried.

Richard Monckton Milnes (1809–85), one of Florence's admirers. They remained friends for life.

An interest in social issues

Florence's parents hoped she would find a suitable partner, have children, entertain guests, and do all the things that were expected of a woman in polite society. Florence went to dances and the theatre, and she loved music. But there was more to life for Florence than music and dancing. She had become interested in social issues, such as poverty and healthcare. Sometimes, when Florence stayed at Lea Hurst, she went to the homes of sick people in the nearby village. She had found an interest in nursing the sick and needy.

A hospital in Germany

Florence longed to meet people with whom she could have intelligent conversations. In 1842 she was introduced to Christian Bunsen, the Prussian **ambassador** to London. He was a **scholar**, and before long Florence was a frequent visitor to his house. She borrowed his books and discussed **archaeology** and religion with him.

People queue outside a hospital in the early 1800s. Seriously ill patients were often turned away, for fear that they would bring infections into hospital.

It was at one of these meetings that he told her about the **Institution of Deaconesses** at the town of Kaiserswerth, near Düsseldorf in Prussia (present-day Germany). The Institution was, in part, a hospital with trained nurses. Florence was fascinated – the idea that nursing was a subject that could be taught was entirely new to her.

In her early 20s Florence started to sense what God's purpose for her was – she was now certain that God wanted her to be a nurse. In 1844, an American **philanthropist**, Dr Samuel Gridley Howe, visited the Nightingale family. Florence asked him if he thought it would be 'a dreadful thing' if she were to devote her life to nursing. He replied that it would be 'a very good thing'. The idea of working in nursing began to take shape in her mind.

This cartoon of the 1840s shows a nurse as an uncaring, untidy woman.

A family row

Florence knew that her parents would not allow her to go to Kaiserswerth, so she did not ask them. Instead, in 1845 she asked if she could visit the nearby hospital in Salisbury. It would only be for three months she said, just long enough for her to learn the day-to-day work of nursing. Florence's parents were horrified. At that time, a hospital was no place for a respectable woman. Florence's mother was ashamed of her and her father thought her education had been wasted. Parthenope was extremely upset. Not surprisingly, Florence was told she could not go.

In Nightingale's words:

'You don't think that I'm going to stay dangling about my mother's drawing room all my life. I shall go out to work, to be sure.'

(From a private note)

Florence goes to Kaiserswerth

Nurses caring for children in the children's ward at Kaiserswerth Hospital, Prussia.

In the 1840s, towns in Britain had poor **sanitation**. Diseases, such as **cholera**, spread quickly. The government looked at the situation and issued regular reports. Florence read them, in secret. Each day, starting before dawn, she made detailed notes of what she learned and produced tables of **statistics** that showed facts and figures at a glance. Florence also wrote to experts in France and Prussia. As her knowledge of sanitation increased she, too, became an expert on the subject. But by breakfast time, in front of her family, Florence became the 'obedient daughter at home' again.

Helpful friends

As the round of house parties and socializing continued, Florence was torn between her family life and the life she wanted for herself. In 1847 she fell ill, with headaches, **bronchitis** and coughs. She feared she was going mad. Family friends, Charles and Selina Bracebridge, suggested she travel with them to Italy. Florence's family thought it would do her good. It did, and for a time she was happy. While in Italy, she met a British politician, Sidney Herbert, and his wife Elizabeth. They became firm friends.

Florence returned home, but it was not long before she was ill once more. After months of feeling low in spirit, the Bracebridges again came to her rescue.

14

Florence went on another foreign tour with them. For Florence, the highlight was travelling in Prussia. The Bracebridges knew that Florence was interested in nursing, and when she said she wanted to visit the hospital at Kaiserswerth they did not try to stop her. Florence arrived there on 31 July 1850. She stayed there for two weeks.

The hospital at Kaiserswerth was founded in 1833 by Pastor Theodor Fliedner. He started it as an orphanage, and it grew to include a school and a hospital. In 1851, when Florence Nightingale trained there, the hospital had beds for 100 patients who were cared for by 27 nurses. Women from all over Prussia went to Kaiserswerth to be trained as nurses. They worked hard, from 5 a.m. until late at night, stopping only to eat and pray.

In Nightingale's words:

'*[Kaiserswerth] is my home, there are my brothers and sisters all at work. There my heart is and there, I trust, will one day be my body.*'

(From a private note in which Florence confided her hopes to visit the hospital at Kaiserswerth)

The Institution of Deaconesses at Kaiserswerth, Prussia. It was here that Florence trained to be a nurse.

Being punished

When Florence's parents discovered that she had been to Kaiserswerth, they were furious. As a punishment, Florence had to work as her sister's servant for six months. Women from wealthy families at the time did not go to work, and remained dependent on their parents until they married. Florence was 30 years old, yet her parents still treated her like a naughty child. In her heart, she knew she could not change the way they felt. She decided to take matters into her own hands. In 1851, after her 'slavery' to Parthenope was over, Florence returned to Kaiserswerth. She went alone and stayed for three months. Whether her parents liked it or not, Florence was going to train to be a nurse.

1 Harley Street, London

Harley Street, London, today. This was where Florence worked as a nurse, in a small hospital.

The reaction from Florence's parents when she returned home from Kaiserswerth was what she expected: 'They would hardly speak to me,' she wrote. Parthenope, who resented her younger sister's growing independence, had a **nervous breakdown**. It was Florence who nursed her back to health.

Independence

In April 1853, Florence's friend, Elizabeth Herbert, wrote to her and told her that a **superintendent** was needed to run the Institution for the Care of Sick Gentlewomen in Distressed Circumstances. This was a small, private hospital in London. Florence was interviewed, and was offered the job. She would have complete control of the hospital, and although she would not be paid, she would be allowed to live on the premises.

The news that Florence had accepted the job caused yet another family argument. Her mother fainted and her sister became terribly upset and was put to bed. Florence's father retreated to his private club. Eventually, however, he decided to help her. He gave her an allowance of £500 a year (about £20,000 by today's standards). It was enough for her to live on. At 33, Florence was finally accepted by her family as an independent adult, and on 12 August 1853 she began her nursing work in earnest.

From house to hospital

The hospital that Florence was to run was moving to new premises, at 1 Harley Street, London. It had been a private house, and Florence had just ten days to turn it into a hospital. She introduced new ideas, such as putting bells by the patients' beds. When a bell was rung, a valve popped open to show the nurse which patient had called for help. Florence's main problem was a shortage of nurses – the women who worked at the hospital had not been properly trained.

Florence worked in Harley Street for fourteen months. It was an important time in her life. Not only did she put her nursing skills to use but she also showed that she was good at organizing.

*Inside a Harley Street doctor's consulting rooms in the 1800s. Two doctors and a **matron** are discussing treatment for a patient.*

War in the Crimea

In March 1854, Britain, France and Turkey declared war on Russia. Their aim was to stop Russia from gaining control of Bulgaria and the Balkans, and from occupying Constantinople (modern Istanbul), in Turkey. A large **peninsula** in southern Russia, almost completely surrounded by inland seas, became the war's main battlefield. The peninsula was called the Crimea, and the war fought there from 1854 to 1856 was the Crimean War.

No one to care for the troops

The British soldiers who fought in the war were transported to the Crimea by troop ships. It was a remote place, about 2400 kilometres (1500 miles) away from Britain. The first troops landed at Varna, a town in Bulgaria. In the dirty conditions of the troops' camp, an **epidemic** of the killer disease **cholera** broke out. From here, the army of 27,000 men was hastily transported across the Black Sea to the Crimea, leaving much-needed medical supplies and provisions behind. The army arrived in the Crimea on 14 September 1854, and six days later fought a Russian army in the Battle of the Alma. It was a British victory, but what should have been cause for national celebration soon became a terrible scandal as people at home learned that sick and injured soldiers had not been properly cared for.

The Crimean peninsula is surrounded by the Black Sea and the Sea of Azov. Today, it is part of the Ukraine.

Reporting the war

The Crimean War was the first war witnessed in detail by photographers and newspaper reporters. It was also the first war in which the **telegraph** was used by reporters to send their **dispatches**, or reports, back to their offices. For the first time, the true horror of war touched people far away from the action as they read about it in their newspapers. Writing in *The Times* on 12 October 1854, war reporter William Russell said: 'It is with feelings of surprise and anger that the public will learn that no sufficient preparations have been made for the care of the wounded. Not only are there not sufficient surgeons… no nurses… there is not even linen to make bandages.'

William Russell, the journalist whose reports in The Times newspaper brought home the horror of war and the conditions of the troops in the Crimea.

Russell's dispatches were highly critical of the British army and they caused shock and outrage. Florence Nightingale read Russell's reports, and understood the need for better medical care in the army. But she could never have predicted how deeply involved she would become.

WILLIAM RUSSELL – WAR REPORTER

Born in Ireland, William Russell (1821–1907) became the world's first official war correspondent when he reported on the Crimean War. He wrote for *The Times*, one of Britain's most respected daily newspapers. After that war, Russell reported on other conflicts around the world, including the American Civil War (1861–65). In 1895 he was knighted by Queen Victoria. From then on he was known as Sir William Russell.

Florence goes to Turkey

The news reports of the Crimean War shocked Britain into action. *The Times* newspaper set up a fund to raise money to buy medical supplies. People wrote angry letters to the newspapers. One letter, to *The Times*, demanded to know why no nurses had been sent to care for the British soldiers.

A government request

The letter was read by Sidney Herbert, Florence's old friend, who was now the government **Secretary-at-War**. Since the news about the dreadful conditions of the troops in the Crimea had become public knowledge, Herbert was under pressure to do something about the situation. On 15 October 1854, he wrote to Florence to ask her, on behalf of the British government, to take charge of the army's hospitals that had been set up in Turkey. He wrote: 'There is but one person in England that I know of who would be capable of organizing and superintending such a scheme.' It was a challenge that Florence readily accepted. She gave up her job at the Harley Street hospital, and began planning for her trip.

SIDNEY HERBERT – POLITICIAN

Born into an **aristocratic** family, Sidney Herbert (1810–61), was elected the Member of Parliament for South Wiltshire when he was only 22 years old. He was a highly capable politician and had special responsibility for the British armed forces. He was the government official (called the Secretary-at-War) in overall charge of the army during the Crimean War. He made important changes that resulted in improved sanitary conditions and education for the forces. In 1861 he became Lord Herbert of Lea.

The journey to Turkey

It was decided that 40 nurses should go with Florence, but only 14 could be found who had any experience of working in hospitals. In the end, Florence gathered together 38 women – a mixture of nurses and nuns. The nurses were to be paid between 12 and 14 shillings per week (60–70p). After a year's good conduct they were to be paid between 18 and 20 shillings (90p–£1). This was much more than hospital nurses in London were paid at the time. Uniforms were quickly made for them, and on 21 October, just one week after Florence had been put in charge, the party left London. They travelled to the port of Marseilles, in the south of France, where they boarded a ship called the *Vectis*. On 4 November, they reached Scutari, a village in Turkey near the Black Sea. It was here that the British army had set up several hospitals for soldiers wounded in the Crimea, about 560 kilometres (350 miles) to the north. This was where Florence was going to work.

The *Vectis* carried Florence and her nurses to Scutari. The ship was infested with cockroaches, and Florence was sea-sick.

In Nightingale's words:

'I do not say that I believe The Times *accounts, but I do believe that we may be of use to the wounded wretches.'*

(From a letter to her friend, Elizabeth Herbert, 14 October 1854)

A hospital at Scutari

The British called their main hospital at Scutari the Barrack Hospital. It had originally been built as a **barracks** for soldiers of the Turkish army, but since the beginning of the Crimean War it had been converted into a hospital for British soldiers. It was run by officials and doctors of the British army. The building was vast – a great square with a tower at each corner. Inside was a warren of rooms laid out along 6.5 kilometres (4 miles) of corridors.

BATTLE OF BALACLAVA

Balaclava, a port in the Crimea, was captured by the British early in the Crimean War. On 25 October 1854, Russian forces attacked the British army at Balaclava, and many soldiers were injured or killed on both sides. The battle became infamous because a misunderstanding of orders sent a British **cavalry regiment** charging straight into the Russian guns. Of the 673 soldiers who took part in the Charge of the Light Brigade, as it came to be known, 272 died. The injured were transported by ship to the Barrack Hospital at Scutari.

In spite of feeling unwell from the sea voyage, Florence was keen to begin her work at the Barrack Hospital as soon as she could. She went to the hospital on 5 November 1854, the day after she had arrived in Turkey. Conditions inside the hospital were far worse than she could ever have imagined. There was no furniture or anything to cook with, rubbish was scattered around, the toilets were blocked, and there were rats everywhere. It was in these dreadful conditions that Florence and her nurses were expected to live and work.

The Barrack Hospital at Scutari, Turkey. Florence sought to improve conditions for soldiers who were patients here.

A factory in Britain, where women made **lint** for dressings. From here it was shipped out to the Crimea.

Conflict with doctors

In her first few days at Scutari, the work that Florence did was not the nursing she had expected. She was not accepted by the male doctors in the hospital. They were in overall charge, and they resented women being sent to work with them. At first, they even refused to allow Florence and her nurses to have anything to do with the patients. The doctors regarded the patients as their responsibility.

In spite of the difficult atmosphere, Florence stayed calm. She set her nurses to cleaning linen, making pillows and preparing slings for broken limbs. Floors were cleaned and the kitchens were tidied up. Then ships began arriving with soldiers who had been wounded at the Battle of Balaclava. The hospital was already filled with about 1700 patients, and room had to be made for the 500 new arrivals. The doctors still believed they could cope on their own.

In Nightingale's words:

'... these colossal calamities, as the hospitals of Scutari will come to be called in history.'

(From a letter to her mother, in which she described the appalling conditions in the hospitals at Scutari, 1 February 1855)

23

The lady with a lamp

Florence Nightingale in the Barrack Hospital at Scutari, painted in 1855.

As the sick and injured from Balaclava were admitted to the Barrack Hospital, it became clear that the doctors could not cope without extra help. Reluctantly, they were forced to admit they needed Florence Nightingale and her nurses. It was time for Florence to begin her real work.

In Nightingale's words:

'As I went my night-rounds among the newly-wounded that first night, there was not one murmur, not one groan.'

(From a letter to her parents, 14 November 1854)

Florence takes charge

To Florence, who was used to neatness and order, the Barrack Hospital was a place of chaos. No one seemed in charge, there were not enough supplies, and the hospital was filthy. The British army officials who should have been running the hospital were overworked and had almost run out of money.

The doctors and hospital officials soon realized that Florence had access to the money raised by *The Times* newspaper, about £30,000 in total. It was enough to buy the supplies they needed. Each day Florence drew up a list of what was needed, and the supplies were bought in the markets at nearby Constantinople.

The goods went into the hospital's stores, and were issued by Florence when she was asked for them. Before long, if anything was needed the best thing to do was to 'go to Miss Nightingale'. Florence's skill at organizing things meant that by December 1854 she was in charge of the hospital's stores. With enough supplies of food, medicine and bedding, conditions for the patients gradually improved.

The soldiers' gratitude

Each night Florence walked the gloomy hospital corridors carrying a lamp to light her way. As the men became used to seeing her they nicknamed her 'the lady with a lamp'. It was a term of affection, which the American poet, Henry Longfellow, used in his poem about Florence Nightingale (page 5). It was said that the men became so devoted to Florence that they even stopped swearing, which they used to do often, and that they kissed her shadow as it passed over them.

Florence carried a Turkish lantern like this. Inside was a single candle whose light shone through the linen sides.

MARY SEACOLE – THE OTHER LADY WITH A LAMP

Mary Seacole (1805–81) was another nurse who cared for the wounded of the Crimean War. Born in Jamaica, she trained as a '**doctress**', like her mother. At her own expense, Mary travelled from Jamaica to the Crimea. On the way, she stopped at Scutari where she met Florence Nightingale. Mary described her as: 'a slight figure... with a pale, gentle and firm face'. From Scutari, Mary went to the Crimea, where she set up the British Hotel, at Balaclava. Sick and **convalescing** soldiers came here to be cared for. Mary fed them, gave them medicine and dressed their wounds. The soldiers called her Mother Seacole. *The Times* newspaper said: 'A more skilful hand about a wound or a broken limb could not be found.'

Changes made by Florence

A hospital kitchen at Scutari, where meals for patients were prepared in bulk.

Florence Nightingale's organizational skills were essential to the running of the Barrack Hospital. She drew up a strict timetable for her nurses. The day began at 8 a.m. with prayers, followed by breakfast. At 9 a.m. a bell rang and they went to the wards, the kitchen or the stores. Work stopped at 2 p.m. for lunch. It began again at 4.30 p.m. and continued until 7 p.m. when there was a break for the evening meal, followed by prayers. Florence said that no nurse should be on the wards after 8 p.m. Night duties were carried out by male **orderlies**. The only nurse seen at night was Florence herself as she patrolled the hospital's corridors. It was not unusual for her to have just four hours' sleep before beginning another long day on duty.

Improved sanitation

Clean sheets and kind words from Florence were not enough to save soldiers from dying. The hospital was still filthy and disease spread quickly. The biggest killer was **cholera**. Florence had been concerned about the hospital's lack of clean water, its blocked toilets and poor drainage.

26

Florence suspected that germs bred and infections spread under these filthy conditions. She pleaded with the authorities. A **Sanitary Commission** was set up to look into the importance of hospital cleanliness. Repairs were made to the drains and the water supply was improved. The death rate fell almost immediately. Before Florence's changes came into force, about 40 per cent of patients died. Afterwards the number of deaths fell to about 2 per cent.

Florence falls ill

In June 1855 conditions at the Barrack Hospital had improved, and Florence visited the Crimea. She inspected field hospitals and went to meet soldiers on the front line. She fell ill with '**Crimean fever**', and there were fears for her life. Florence recovered, but instead of returning to Britain she went back to Scutari to continue her work there. It was only when the war ended, in March 1856, that Florence felt free to leave, and she returned to Britain that August.

Alexis Soyer, the chef.

ALEXIS SOYER – HOSPITAL CHEF

The food ration each day for a British soldier was 1 lb (about half a kilo) of meat and bread, with a little coffee, sugar, salt and water. There were few vegetables. At Scutari, a French chef called Alexis Soyer (1809–58) was invited by Florence to devise nourishing meals for the patients. In particular, they were fed beef and mutton soups. Soyer trained soldiers to work as cooks, and taught them to prepare meals in bulk, so they could cook for thousands of patients at a time.

A national heroine

In Nightingale's words:

'The publicity and talk there have been about this work [at Scutari] have injured it more than anything else, and in no way... will I contribute by making a show of myself.'

(From a private note, outlining her reasons for shunning the public, August 1856)

Florence Nightingale's work in the Crimea became well known in Britain. Soldiers spoke of her with great affection, and the government praised her. Sidney Herbert, the official who had asked her to take charge of the army's hospitals in Turkey, called her a 'diamond'. Florence had become a national heroine, but she did not want publicity.

A royal request

When Florence returned to Britain, she moved back in with her parents and sister. Florence received thousands of letters. There were letters from men asking Florence to marry them, letters begging for money, and some with strange requests – one man asked her to give him a donkey! Parthenope often replied to these letters on Florence's behalf. Florence was asked to speak at meetings and accept awards, but she refused them all. However, there was one invitation she could not turn down – a request to meet Queen Victoria. In September 1856, Florence met her at Balmoral, the queen's Scottish home.

Queen Victoria awarded Florence this brooch, which was designed by Prince Albert. It was to thank Florence for her work in caring for the 'Queen's brave soldiers'.

Many people would have been stuck for words, but Florence knew exactly what to say. She spoke softly and clearly about the problems in the army's hospital system, especially the poor standards of **hygiene** and diet. The queen listened, and agreed with Florence. With the queen on her side, there would be little to prevent Florence from getting exactly what she believed was needed. Florence wanted a **Royal Commission** to be set up to investigate the health of the British army. She was determined to **reform** how the army cared for sick and wounded men.

Another illness

In 1857 Florence fell ill. She felt tired and weak, and lost weight. She was told she was working too hard and should rest. At the time no one could say what her illness was. Florence referred to it as her 'thorn in the flesh'. Today, some doctors believe she was suffering from the after-effects of seeing terrible pain and suffering during the Crimean War. Doctors today call this condition **post-traumatic stress disorder**.

A pottery model of Florence and a wounded soldier. Figures like this were bought by ordinary people as souvenirs of their heroine.

POST-TRAUMATIC STRESS DISORDER

Post-traumatic stress disorder (PTSD) affects people after they have experienced a life-threatening event. This can be war, a natural disaster, a serious accident or a personal assault. PTSD sufferers relive their experience through nightmares and flashbacks, have difficulty sleeping, and feel detached from everyday life. They have headaches, stomach complaints, and feel dizzy. Research has shown that women are more likely to suffer from PTSD than men.

Florence's 1000-page report was called Notes on Matters Affecting the Health, Efficiency and Hospital Administration of the British Army.

A **Royal Commission** was set up to examine the health of the British army. Florence selected men who were experts in subjects such as **statistics** and **sanitation** to work for the Commission (there were no women Commissioners). Sidney Herbert, Florence's good friend, was the chairman.

Prevention is better than cure

In 1858, Florence published the results of her investigation. Her report contained almost 1000 pages, crammed with facts and statistics. The report looked at the way in which the British army had organized its hospitals during wars and also in peace-time. Page after page told the same sad story – that most of the army's deaths, in war and in peace, were caused by poor **hygiene**. Florence noted that army doctors were trained to work as surgeons. They were not trained to prevent disease. Florence decided that prevention is better than cure. She said that soldiers should be given good food, clothing and shelter, and that they should live in clean, hygienic conditions. If the army treated its men well, they were less likely to fall ill. Florence had gathered information about the main diseases that affected the army, particularly infectious ones that spread in dirty conditions, such as **cholera**, **typhoid** and **dysentery**. She knew that improved hygiene and better organization of the army's camps, **barracks** and hospitals could prevent these diseases from occurring.

Florence's flair for mathematics was put to good use. She used statistics to prepare diagrams that showed the causes of death among the soldiers who had served in the Crimean War.

PARTHENOPE'S MARRIAGE

In 1858, Parthenope, Florence's sister, married Sir Harry Verney and became Lady Verney. Parthenope was 39 years old. They lived in a mansion called Claydon House, in Buckinghamshire. Parthenope became a popular hostess and rich and important people came to her parties. She wrote stories and some were printed in magazines.

British soldiers at rest in army barracks in India.

Her statistical charts showed at a glance that most troops had died from preventable diseases. While 4500 had been killed or died of wounds, a staggering 17,600 had died of disease.

Army officials saw that drastic changes were needed. As a direct result of Florence's work, by 1860 an Army Medical School had been established, and the hygiene of the army's **barracks** and hospitals had been improved.

Concerns for India

Florence's pioneering work was felt as far away as India (which was ruled by Britain at the time), where **regiments** of the British army were stationed. Improvements in hygiene were made there, too, and for the rest of her life Florence remained interested in the state of India's sanitation. Though she never visited India, she wrote reports and issued guidelines that helped the nation to improve the health of its population.

In Nightingale's words:

'No one can feel for the army as I do. People must have seen that long dreadful winter to know what it was. I can never forget.'

(From a letter to her sister, Parthenope, March 1856)

The Nightingale Nurses

Florence was always busy working on new ideas. One idea had been with her since before she went to Turkey. She had thought about setting up a training school for nurses, but there was little she could do about it while she was away from Britain. In spite of this, a meeting was held in her absence.

THE NIGHTINGALE FUND.

THE signal services rendered by Miss NIGHTINGALE, to the sick and wounded of the British Forces in the East, have excited throughout the country a universal desire to testify by some marked and substantial acknowledgment, the gratitude and admiration of the British people.

But Miss NIGHTINGALE has nobly refused to accept any testimonial from which she could derive personal advantage of any description; while it is ascertained that the tribute most in harmony with her feelings and wishes, would be to afford further scope for her disinterested exertions by placing under her immediate superintendance the establishment of an Institution for the reception, protection, and training, of Hospital Nurses and Assistants, whereby the inestimable blessings of the system she has introduced, may be perpetuated and extended generally to the Poor, who may be suffering from sickness or accident.

To effect this object a public appeal has been made, to which the noble, the wealthy, and the benevolent, have liberally responded. But it is felt, that opportunity should not be denied to any class to manifest the sympathy all are known to entertain towards their devoted and highminded Countrywoman. The contributions, however small, of those who are dependent upon their labor, will have a peculiar fitness when given for an object by which the necessitous are to be exclusively benefited; while it is certain the widow's mite will have equal value in the estimation of Miss NIGHTINGALE, with the largest gifts of the great and the affluent.

Partaking in these views, the Proprietors of this Establishment have given permission for a Subscription Book to be opened in the Counting House where any contributions however small, will be received and recorded; and the amount collected will be transmitted to the Committee and advertised as the contribution of the Workmen and others in this Establishment.

December 29th 1855.

A poster explaining the purpose of the Nightingale Fund. It was displayed in banks, and handed out at station bookstalls.

The Nightingale Fund

About 9 months before Florence returned from the Crimea, more than 1000 people had squeezed into a hall in London. They had come to hear plans to set up a fund, called the Nightingale Fund, to raise money for the training of nurses. Within three weeks 20,000 letters had been sent out asking for money. The highest contribution from a single person was £300. By June 1856, £44,039 had been raised (about £2 million in today's money). The fund also increased people's awareness that nursing was a suitable occupation for respectable, educated women, and that nurses needed to be properly trained.

The Nightingale Training School

St Thomas's Hospital, London, was chosen as the site for the new training school. Florence had been impressed by the **Matron** there, Mrs Sarah Wardroper, and felt she was the only person who could take charge of the nurses' training.

On 24 June 1860, nearly four years after Florence's return to Britain, the first group of fifteen trainee nurses, called **probationers**, began their training at the Nightingale Training School. The nurses who studied there became known as Nightingale Nurses.

Mrs Sarah Wardroper, the Matron at St Thomas's Hospital, chosen by Florence to train the first Nightingale Nurses.

They trained for a year, had their own rooms, and were provided with brown uniforms and white caps and aprons. When their training was over, they were sent to work in hospitals in Britain and abroad. Some set up new schools to teach nursing.

In Nightingale's words:

'The Matron of that hospital is the only one of any existing hospital that I would recommend to form a school for nurses. It will be a beginning in a very humble way.'

(From a letter to Sidney Herbert, indicating that St Thomas's Hospital should be the place for the first school for nurses, 24 May 1859)

SARAH WARDROPER

Sarah Wardroper began nursing when she was 42 years old. She had no training, but, like Florence Nightingale, she had a will to succeed. She worked at St Thomas's Hospital in London, and in 1853 she became its Matron. She improved the standard of nursing at the hospital.

The Nightingale Training School owed much to Florence, yet once it was established she had little to do with it. She only ever visited it once, in 1886, but every year for thirty years she wrote a letter to the nurses giving advice and encouragement.

Florence the writer

It has been estimated that Florence wrote 13,000 letters, and more than 200 articles, pamphlets, reports and books – in addition to all the private notes she had written since childhood. At the end of 1859 she brought out a short book called *Notes on Nursing: What it is, and what it is not*. With a title like that no one had any doubts what it was about, and it became a bestseller.

The pages of *Notes on Nursing* were filled with Florence's wisdom, based on her experience of nursing. Only she had the first-hand knowledge to write such a book. She did not intend it to be a nurse's instruction manual. In the book's preface she wrote: 'I do not pretend to teach her how, I ask her to teach herself, and for this purpose I venture to give her some hints'. Florence, as ever, was being modest, and the nurses who read the book cannot have failed to learn from it.

*For my dear Beatrice from her loving Flo.
New Year's Day 1860*

NOTES ON NURSING:

WHAT IT IS, AND WHAT IT IS NOT.

BY

FLORENCE NIGHTINGALE.

LONDON:
HARRISON, 59, PALL MALL,
BOOKSELLER TO THE QUEEN.

Notes on Nursing, *Florence's most famous book. It has been translated into many foreign languages.*

In Nightingale's words:

'The fidget of silk and crinoline, the rattling of keys, the creaking of stays [corsets] and of shoes, will do a patient more harm than all the medicines in the world will do him good.'

(From the chapter 'Noise'; *Notes on Nursing*, 1859)

Observation and sensitivity

Notes on Nursing contained chapters with titles such as 'Health of Houses', 'Personal Cleanliness', 'What Food?' and 'Bed and Bedding'. It outlined two of the most important principles of nursing – observation and sensitivity to a patient's needs. Observation, said Florence, was how the nurse gathered her facts. The nurse should observe things about a patient such as pulse, appetite and breathing. A patient's comforts were also very important – a nurse had to make sure the patient was not too hot or too cold, that the ward was not too noisy, and that there was plenty of fresh air. Much of what Florence wrote seems like common sense today, yet people at the time needed to be told about it.

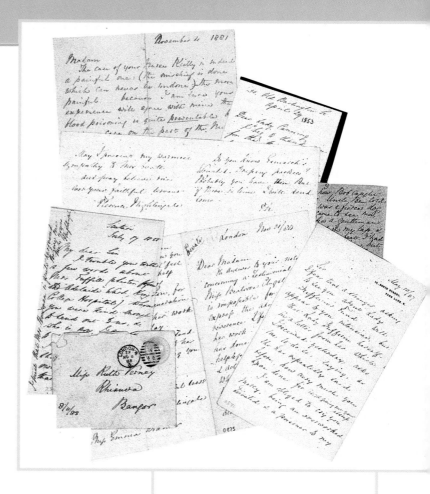

Letters written by Florence. She wrote neatly with a steel-nibbed pen dipped in ink.

DOROTHEA DIX – AN AMERICAN NURSE

The 1860s saw the beginning of nursing as a profession in the USA. It was based on the pioneering work of Florence Nightingale. During the American Civil War (1861–65), Dorothea Dix (1802–87) became **Superintendent** of Female Nurses. She was in charge of all women nurses working in army hospitals of the Union (the states in the north of the United States). Dorothea, like Florence, was opposed by male doctors, but she was able to convince them of the importance of nurses. She recruited more than 3000 nurses during the Civil War.

Florence's nurses

Florence aged 66, photographed with a group of Nightingale Nurses in 1886.

In Nightingale's words:

'Let us hail the successes of other Training Schools, sprung up, thank God, so fast and well in latter years.'

(From a letter to trainees, 1884)

Every ten years a **census** is held in Britain to find out how many people there are in the country, where they live, and what work they do. At the back of Florence's book *Notes on Nursing* she included information from the 1851 census. It showed there were 25,466 women in Britain who said they worked as nurses. But what the census could not show was how good these nurses were at their work. Some may well have been the so-called 'old style' nurses who had given nursing a poor reputation before Florence's **reforms**. 'Old style' nurses were untrained workers who knew little about nursing. They were criticized for being untidy and uncaring, sometimes doing more harm than good. Florence's fascination with **statistics** was, once again, put to good use. She used the census information to show that nursing was an occupation for older women. In 1851 most nurses were aged between 50 and 60 – and 147 were over 85!

This is the timetable for trainee nurses at the Nightingale Training School in 1862:

DAY DUTY										
6 a.m.	6.30 a.m.	7 a.m.	1 p.m.	2 p.m.	3.30 p.m.	5 p.m.	6 p.m.	8.30 p.m.	9 p.m.	10 p.m.
Rise	Breakfast	Wards	Dinner	Wards	Exercise	Tea	Wards	Dormitory	Supper	Bed

NIGHT DUTY										
9 p.m.	9.30 p.m.	10 p.m.	6 a.m.	6.30 a.m.	7 a.m.	10 a.m.	11 a.m.	1 p.m.	2 p.m.
Rise	Tea	Wards	Dormitory	Breakfast	Wards	Dormitory	Exercise	Dinner	Bed

The first Nightingale Nurses

The fifteen trainee nurses who entered the Nightingale Training School in June 1860 were younger women, aged between 22 and 40. They had been chosen because of their seemingly good characters. However, four were asked to leave before the end of their year's training – one because of illness, two because they had been disobedient, and one for drunkenness! Since Florence intended to make nursing a respectable, modern profession, drinking alcohol while on duty had to stop. It belonged to the bad days of 'old-style' nursing.

Florence drew up a personal record sheet for every trainee. The **Matron**, Mrs Wardroper, filled it in, noting such things as the trainee's punctuality, trustworthiness, cleanliness and honesty. The trainee's nursing skills in bandaging, making beds, applying medicinal leeches (blood-sucking worms used to extract patients' blood), and observing the sick were also noted. Florence knew that if her reforms were to succeed, her nurses must be good at their work, and have good characters, too.

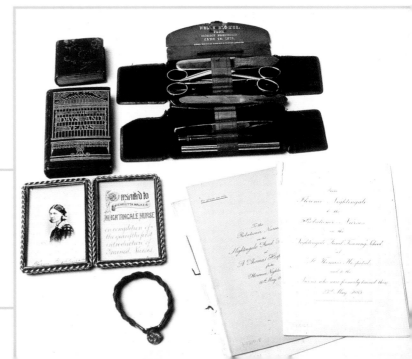

Florence gave gifts, such as books and nursing instruments, to the nurses who trained at the Nightingale Training School.

Florence and St Thomas's Hospital

Florence began her long association with St Thomas's Hospital in 1860, when it became home to the Nightingale Training School. At one time she imagined she would spend the rest of her life at the hospital, living quietly into old age in a side room. But this was not to be.

Florence's London home

Since Florence's return to Britain from the Crimea in 1856, she had never had a home of her own. Instead, she had lived in hotels, in rented rooms, and in her parents' homes at Embley Park and Lea Hurst. All this changed in 1865, when her father bought her a house in the centre of London, at 10 South Street. Florence settled in with servants to help her, and cats for company. A room in her home was also her office.

A new Nightingale Training School

Meanwhile, St Thomas's Hospital had continued to expand, and by the late 1860s it had outgrown its premises. It was decided to build a new hospital. Florence was in her late 40s, and she regarded herself as old. Despite poor health, she took an interest in the design of the building. She was determined that the new hospital should be built to the highest, most **hygienic** standards of the day. In 1868 Queen Victoria laid the foundation stone for the new hospital. Florence was too ill to attend.

> ### In Nightingale's words:
>
> *'It is always cheaper to build a good hospital than a bad one.'*
>
> (From a letter to her brother-in-law, Sir Harry Verney)

St Thomas's Hospital as it looked from the outside during the late 1800s.

Three years later, in June 1871, when the building was completed, the queen returned to declare the new St Thomas's open. It had been given a larger Nightingale Training School, which Florence said should be much more than a place of study. She wanted it to be a 'home' for the nurses who lived and trained there. Florence arranged for the trainee nurses to attend Bible classes and listen to music, and encouraged them to read popular books of the day. She wanted to broaden their educations.

A ward at St Thomas's Hospital in 1890. The wide spacing of the beds was one of the changes brought about by Florence's **reforms**.

LINDA RICHARDS – FIRST TRAINED NURSE IN THE USA

The first training school for nurses in America was established in the early 1870s in Boston. The first nurse to qualify there was Linda Richards (1841–1930), recognized as America's first trained nurse. Linda went on to work at the Bellevue Hospital, New York City, where she met Sister Helen, a nun who had trained in London as a Nightingale Nurse. In 1877, Linda studied at St Thomas's Hospital, London. During her six months in Britain she met Florence Nightingale and visited other hospitals. She used her experience to set up nurse training schools in America and Japan.

Florence's last years

By the 1870s Florence's most important work had been done. Her busy life slowed down as the reforms she had begun in nursing and hospitals became standard practice, and as other people carried on her work.

Still helping

In 1874, Florence's father died. For the next six years Florence was cut off from her work while she cared for her elderly and infirm mother, whom she nursed at Lea Hurst, the family home in Derbyshire. Her mother died there in 1880. Florence, then aged 60, returned to London, to her house in South Street.

In spite of her age and poor health, Florence still wanted to help people. Her doctor had told her to rest for a year, but for Florence this was impossible to do – she had given her life to serving the needy and she could not stop now. Ignoring her doctor's instructions, Florence resumed her work. She watched over the Nightingale Training School; she renewed her interest in India and the health of the people who lived there, and she became interested in the health of the British army in Africa. Florence's sister, Parthenope, suffered from arthritis later in life. Florence helped to care for her until she died in 1890. For as long as she could, Florence was determined to help others.

This photograph of Florence was taken when she was 71 years old.

Failing health

Florence began to lose her eyesight when she was in her 80s. In 1901 she went blind. Her memory began to fail, too. She was cared for at home. Visitors still called to see her, and the government sometimes asked for her advice on matters to do with public health.

In old age, Florence received many awards. In 1907, King Edward VII gave her the **Order of Merit** – a great honour for a British citizen. Florence was the first woman ever to receive it, given to her 'in recognition of invaluable services to the country and to humanity'. The next year she was granted the **Freedom of the City** of London. Women who had been christened 'Florence' in her honour sent letters, and old soldiers who had fought in the Crimean War said they had never forgotten her.

A message of congratulations to Florence from the nurses of South Australia, 1904.

Florence died peacefully on 13 August 1910, aged 90. She was buried in the family grave in the village of East Wellow, Hampshire. On the day of the funeral a service was held in St Paul's Cathedral, London, attended by **veterans** of the Crimean War and 1000 nurses. They had come to remember the 'lady with a lamp'. For them, and for countless thousands of others across the world, its flame would never die.

The legacy of Florence Nightingale

Before Florence Nightingale pushed for change in the hospitals of the British army, nursing was a disorganized profession. Nurses' lack of training often did more harm than good. Florence made it her life's work to **reform** nursing and healthcare. She looked at the way hospitals were run and studied facts carefully to develop an improved system of nursing. She turned nursing into the respectable profession it is today.

A legacy of change

One of Florence Nightingale's greatest reforms was that she created new ways of working for nurses. Today's nurses do their jobs effectively and efficiently because Florence considered nurses' needs.

Florence also raised standards of care to a high level. Today's nurses are professional people whose duty it is to give patients the best possible care. Florence pioneered the use of **statistics** and graphs in healthcare.

These forms of communication are regularly used today to see at a glance changes in the condition of a patient. Florence showed how observation, carefully watching patients for signs of their needs, was a key feature of nursing. Nurses today routinely monitor and manage their patients' needs, checking up on them regularly.

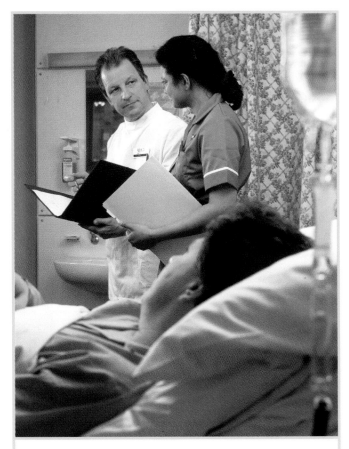

Men as well as women work as hospital nurses today.

In Nightingale's words:

'When I am no longer even a memory, just a name, I hope my voice may perpetuate the great work of my life. God bless my dear old comrades of Balaclava and bring them safe to shore.'

(A sound recording of Florence's voice was made in London in 1890. These are her only recorded spoken words.)

She demonstrated that a healthy environment was good for a patient, and that comforting and caring for a patient is at the centre of all good healthcare. This is as true today as it was in Florence's time.

Florence showed how healthcare reforms can come about as the result of like-minded people working together to solve a problem. Nothing is ever finished, and what Florence began is continually being improved by her successors today in hospitals around the world. She believed in the need to train nurses. Today's nurses are trained in schools of nursing. After qualifying, nurses regularly attend courses to bring them up-to-date with the latest nursing practices and methods.

Today's nurses are highly-skilled people.

Florence's attention to detail was incredible. She did not stop at improving nurses' skills, she also influenced the design of hospitals. Today's buildings are partly the result of Florence's ideas. They are built from **hygienic** materials, and wards are designed so that a nurse can see every patient easily.

Florence Nightingale influenced healthcare around the world in the 19th and 20th centuries. Her achievements are even greater when we consider that she was working at a time when society was not used to women who were capable reformers. All this adds up to a huge legacy. Now, in the first years of the 21st century, the lessons learned from Florence's work are as relevant as they were then.

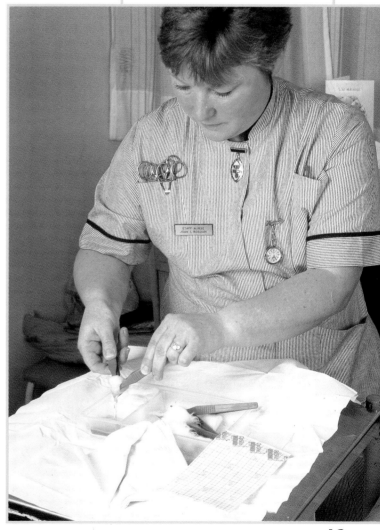

Timeline

1820	Florence Nightingale born in Florence, Italy.
1821	Florence returns to Britain with her family.
	They settle in Derbyshire in a new house called Lea Hurst.
1825	The family move to a larger house, Embley Park, Hampshire.
	Florence's father begins to educate her at home.
1837	Florence believes she hears the voice of God.
	She travels to Europe with her family.
1839	Florence returns to Britain and 'comes out'.
1842	Meets Richard Monckton Milnes.
	Learns about the hospital at Kaiserswerth, Prussia.
1844	Asks a family friend about devoting her life to nursing.
	Declines a proposal of marriage from Henry Nicholson.
1845	Parents refuse to let her train to be a nurse at Salisbury Infirmary.
1846	Starts to become a self-taught expert on hospitals and sanitation.
1847	Falls ill and is close to having a nervous breakdown.
	Goes to Italy with Charles and Selina Bracebridge.
	Meets Sidney and Elizabeth Herbert.
1849	Declines to marry Richard Monckton Milnes.
	Close to another nervous breakdown, she again travels abroad with the Bracebridges.
1850	Her first visit to the hospital at Kaiserswerth.
1851	Returns to Kaiserswerth and stays for three months, training to be a nurse.
1853	Given a yearly allowance of £500 by her father.
	Accepts her first job, as Superintendent of the Institution for the Care of Sick Gentlewomen in Distressed Circumstances, London.
1854	Crimean War begins.
	Asked by Sidney Herbert, the government Secretary-at-War, to take charge of the army's hospitals in Turkey.
	Travels to the Barrack Hospital at Scutari, Turkey.
1855	Visits the Crimea where she contracts 'Crimean fever'.
	Plans are made, in London, to set up the Nightingale Fund.
1856	Crimean War ends and Florence returns to Britain.
	Meets Queen Victoria and Prince Albert.
1857	Gathers a huge amount of information on the health of the army.
	Becomes aware of the need to improve the public health of India.
1858	Publishes *Notes on Matters Affecting the Health, Efficiency and Hospital Administration of the British Army*.

1859	Publishes a small book called *Notes on Nursing*.
1860	Nightingale Training School for nurses opens at St Thomas's Hospital, London.
	Army Medical College opens, at Chatham, Kent.
	Florence is the first woman to be elected a Fellow of the Statistical Society.
1865	Florence moves to 10 South Street, London.
1874	Father dies.
1880	Mother dies.
1883	Florence is awarded the Royal Red Cross.
1890	Sister dies.
1907	Florence becomes the first woman to receive the Order of Merit.
1908	Given the Freedom of the City of London.
1910	Death of Florence Nightingale.

Places to visit and further reading

Places to visit

The Florence Nightingale Museum, London, England

The Nightingale family memorial (Florence's grave), St Margaret's Church, East Wellow, Hampshire, England

Websites

Website of the Florence Nightingale Museum:
  www.florence-nightingale.co.uk/

Tribute website containing a sound recording of her voice:
  www.countryjoe.com/nightingale/index.html

Further reading

Ardagh, Philip: *Get a Life! 4: Florence Nightingale* (Macmillan Children's Books, London, 1999)

Burns, Peggy: *Florence Nightingale* (Hodder Wayland, London, 1998)

Fishel, Emma: *Florence Nightingale* (Franklin Watts, London, 1997)

Glossary

ambassador someone who represents one country's government to that of another country

archaeology study of the past by examining the remains of ancient civilizations and cultures

aristocrat person who belongs to the upper class, who is usually wealthy and who owns land

barracks building or group of buildings used to house soldiers

bronchitis disease, not usually fatal, which affects a person's air-passages and lungs, causing coughs, colds and fevers

cavalry soldiers who ride and fight on horseback

census headcount of the population. A census is carried out in Britain every 10 years

cholera disease, often fatal, spread by infected water which causes diarrhoea, sickness, pains and thirst

'coming out' time at which a girl in her late teens or early twenties was presented by her parents at parties, signifying her passage from childhood to adulthood

convalescing process of recovering after an illness or accident

'Crimean fever' general name given to a number of diseases which affected people during the Crimean War

deaconess Christian woman whose duties are to serve the needs of a community, offering help with things such as healthcare and education

dispatches communications sent by a reporter to a newspaper

doctress woman doctor who heals the sick, especially in societies that believe in the healing powers of plants and minerals

dysentery disease causing sever diarrhoea

epidemic when a great number of people in one place are affected by the same disease at the same time

Freedom of the City honour given to a person by a British city in recognition for services to the country

governess woman who educates children in their own home

hygiene science of protecting people's health through cleanliness

lint linen or cotton material used for dressing wounds

matron woman in charge of nursing at a hospital

nervous breakdown when a person cannot cope with the pressures of daily life, and becomes withdrawn

Order of Merit an award to a British citizen from the king or queen in recognition of services to the country and to humanity; the person is entitled to use the letters OM after their name

orderly attendant who works in a hospital

peninsula piece of land almost completely surrounded by water

philosophy use of reason rather than experimentation to find the truth

philanthropist wealthy person who gives money to good causes for the benefit of others

post-traumatic stress disorder condition experienced by people after they have witnessed or been involved in a life threatening event

prejudice when someone has already made up their mind about something or someone without knowing all the facts

privileged wealthy and fortunate

probationer name given to a trainee nurse at the Nightingale Training School

reform change the way things are done

reformer person who seeks to change things for the better

regiment largest unit of an army, made up of many smaller units called battalions

Royal Commission major inquiry set up by the government designed to investigate something of national importance

sanitation process of protecting public health by improving things such as drainage and the disposal of rubbish

Sanitary Commission inquiry set up by the government to investigate public health

scholar student; also a well-educated, clever person

Secretary-at-War in Victorian Britain, the government minister with responsibility for the armed forces

statistics gathering together and studying numbers

superintendent person who has overall control of a building and the people who work within it

telegraph system for transmitting messages using electricity

typhoid infectious fever caused by bacteria. The patient develops a rash and irritation of the intestines

veteran old soldier

Index

Titles in the *Groundbreakers* series include:

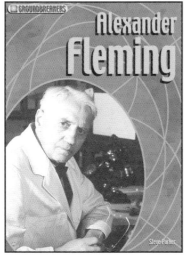

Hardback 0 431 10477 8

Hardback 0 431 10474 3

Hardback 0 431 10475 1

Hardback 0 431 10478 6

Hardback 0 431 10476 X

Hardback 0 431 10479 4

Find out about the other titles in this series on our website www.heinemann.co.uk/library